AF251937

VIRGIN AND STATUE WORSHIP QUIZZES TO A STREET PREACHER

1. Why do you Catholics worship Mary as a goddess?

It would be mortal sin for any Catholic to regard Mary as a **goddess.** If a Catholic expressed such a belief to a priest in Confession he would be refused absolution unless he promised to renounce such as an absurd idea. If you wish to attack Catholic doctrine, at least find out what Catholics do believe before you begin. We Catholics do not give **worship** to Mary, the Mother of Christ, but what we do give to her is the best that we can in the giving, namely, **homage, veneration, reverence,** but never worship. We have enough intelligence to know that Mary the woman who gave human bone, human flesh, and human feature to the Savior of Mankind was not a goddess but a human member of the human race. Although she is a member of our race we hail her as the First Lady of Heaven and of Earth.

2. The genealogies of Christ as given by the Gospel afford one much difficulty. If Jesus was not the son of Joseph, why is His genealogy traced through Joseph?

Jesus was not the natural son of Joseph. But Mary, who was the Mother of Jesus, was related to Joseph, whose genealogy was also her own. It was a Jewish custom to record descent only through the male line.

3. If you call her Queen of Heaven do you not do her an injustice in refusing to her the title of goddess?

It would be the greatest possible injustice to regard her as a goddess. It is just to honor her even as God has honored her, which we Catholics do. Jesus is King of kings and Lord of lords, and His mother certainly possesses **queenly dignity,** holding the highest place in Heaven next to her Divine Son. But that does not, and cannot change her finite and created human nature. To regard her as a goddess would be absurd.

4. Yet you insist that she is the Mother of God!

Jesus Christ is true God and true man, and as He was born of Mary she is truly the Mother of God. The Second Person of the Blessed Trinity was born of her according to the humanity He derived from her. She is not a goddess, for God did not take His Divine Being from her. But she is the Mother of God since the Second Person of the Blessed Trinity was truly born of her in His human nature.

5. How could Mary be the mother of the One who created her?

Mary owed her being, of course, to God, but this under

the aspect of His eternal nature. Subsequent to her creation that human nature was born of her which the Son of God had assumed to Himself. She was, therefore, the mother of Christ. But Christ was one Divine Person existing in **two** natures, one **eternal** and **divine;** the other, **temporal** and **human.** Mary necessarily gave birth to a being with one personality and that divine, and she is rightly called the Mother of God.

6. Does not the Catholic Church insist also upon the biologically impossible dogma of the Immaculate Conception of Mary herself?

The dogma of the Immaculate Conception of Mary has nothing to do with biology. It does not mean that she was conceived miraculously in the physical sense. She was **normally** conceived and born of her parents, Joachim and Ann. But in her very conception her soul was **preserved** immaculate in the sense that she inherited no stain of original sin, derived from our first parents.

7. According to Catholic doctrine the Sacrament of Baptism destroys original sin. Would you say that Mary did not need Baptism?

Mary did not need Baptism insofar as that sacrament was instituted for the destruction of original sin. She received that sacrament in order to participate in its other effects, and chiefly in order to receive the Christian character which that sacrament impresses upon the soul. Mary was not the only one born into this world **free of original sin.** Jeremias, the prophet, picked out by God to preach penance to the Chosen People of God, was sanctified by the action of God, whilst being carried in the womb of his mother so that when he was born he was free of original sin. Jer. I, 5. St. John the Baptist was likewise sanctified in the womb of his mother Elizabeth because he was picked out by God to point out to mankind the Lamb of God, the Messiah, Luke I, 41. Jeremias and St. John were conceived in original sin but before birth were cleansed of original sin. Mary was never conceived in original sin and thus it is only by this privilege that she was never **under the dominion** of the evil spirit. It is only by the privilege of the Immaculate Conception that Mary can be the woman of whom God speaks in prophecy to Satan after the fall of the first parents, Adam and Eve, when He says to the serpent: "Because thou hast done this. . . . I will put enmities between thee and the woman, and between thy seed and her seed; she shall crush thy head, and thou shalt lie in wait for her heel." Gen. III, 14-15.

8. If Mary was sinless she could not have needed redemption! Yet is not Christ the Redeemer of every child of Adam?

Insofar as the sin of Adam involved the whole human race in condemnation Mary needed redeeming. But there are two ways of redeeming. God could allow one to be born in sin and then purify the soul by **subsequent** application of the merits of Christ, or He could, by an **anticipation** of the merits of Christ, exempt a soul from any actual contraction of original sin. Thus He **exempted** Mary from any actual inheritance of the sin, and she owes her exemption to the anticipated merits of Christ. In other words, she was redeemed by Christ by **prevention** rather than by subsequent purification.

9. Is there any evidence in Scripture that Mary was indeed never actually subject to original sin?

Yes. In Gen. III., 15, God said to Satan, "I will put enmities between thee and the woman . . . thou shalt lie in wait for her heel." The radical enmity between Satan and that second Eve, the Mother of Christ, forbids her having been under the dominion of Satan, as she would have been had she ever contracted original sin in actual fact. In Lk. I., 28, we read how the Angel was sent by God to salute Mary with the words, "Hail, full of grace." Grace excludes sin, and had there been any sin at all in Mary she could not have been declared to be **filled with grace.** The Protestant version translates the phrase as "thou that hast been highly favored." But the Greek certainly implies "completely filled with holiness." However, complaints that our doctrine exempts Mary from the contracting of original sin are becoming more and more rare in a world which is tending to **deny** original sin altogether, and which wishes to exempt everybody from it.

10. St. Paul says that one died for all, and therefore all were dead. 2 Cor. V, 14-15.

Such texts must be interpreted in the light of other passages where God reveals that Mary was **never** under the dominion of Satan. Mary is included in these words of St. Paul **juridically** insofar as she was born of Adam, but she was not allowed to be born in sin to be afterwards redeemed. She was redeemed by prevention.

11. St. John knew the Mother of Christ better than the others, yet he does not mention her Immaculate Conception!

In Rev. XII. he shows clearly his knowledge of the deadly opposition between Mary and Satan. His Gospel he wrote to supplement the Synoptic accounts, and sufficient details had been given concerning Mary herself by St. Luke. Omission to mention a fact in a given book is not proof that the writer did not know of it, and above all if it does not fall within the scope of his work.

12. Did the early Church know anything of this doctrine?

St. Augustine, in the **fourth** century wrote: "When it is a matter of sin we must except the holy Virgin Mary, concerning whom I will have no question raised, owing to the honor due to our Lord." St. Ephrem, also in the **fourth** century, taught very clearly the Immaculate Conception of Mary, likening her to Eve before the fall. The Oriental Churches celebrated the feast of the Immaculate Conception as early as the **seventh** century. When Pope Pius IX defined the Catholic doctrine in 1854 he gave, not a **new truth** to be added to Christian teaching, but merely defined that this doctrine was **part of Christian** teaching from the very beginning, and that it is to be believed by all as part of Christian revelation.

13. Your infallible Church allowed St. Bernard to remain in ignorance of this doctrine.

Since the Church had not then given any infallible definition on the subject St. Bernard naturally could not be guided by it. St. Bernard believed that Mary was born **free from sin,** but he was puzzled as to the **moment** of her sanctification. He thought the probable explanation to be that she was conceived in sin, but purified as was St. John the Baptist prior to her actual birth. But he did not regard this opinion as part of his Faith. Meantime his error was immaterial prior to the final authentic decision of the infallible Church. St. Bernard believed all that God had taught and all that the Catholic Church had clearly set forth in her definitions prior to his time.

14. Did not St. Thomas Aquinas deny the doctrine of the Immaculate Conception?

His opinion was probably much the same as that of St. Bernard. Before the **definite decision** of the Church was given theologians were free to discuss the matter. But the Church has since defined that the soul of Mary was never subject for a single moment to the stain of original sin. Both St. Bernard and St. Thomas would have been very glad to have had the assistance of such a definition.

15. Why did the Church withhold that honor from Mary for so long a time?

Since Mary always possessed that honor the Church did not **withhold** it from her. The definition that Mary did possess such an honor was given by the Church when necessity **demanded** it. There was no real dispute about this matter in the early Church. In the middle ages theologians attempted a deeper analysis of the privileges of Mary, and with no infallible decision of the Church to help them, some theologians arrived at defective conclusions chiefly because of the defective psychology of the times. Some theologians held that Mary was preserved from original sin from the very moment of her **conception;** others said from the moment of her **animation;** yet others that she was purified at a moment subsequent both to her conception and to her animation. All admitted that she was sanctified **prior** to her actual birth. Now that the Church has spoken there is no doubt on the subject.

16. Did not Franciscans and Dominicans attack each other bitterly over the Immaculate Conception?

They indulged in much controversy, but it was a free matter for discussion until the Church had given her definite ruling. The Catholic Church demands unity in doctrines which have been **definitely decided,** liberty in matters still undecided, and charity always. I admit that her ideals of charity have not always been maintained by her wayward children in theological controversies, but that is no fault of the Church.

17. Did not Philip III. and Philip IV. ask the Popes Paul V., Gregory V., and Alexander VII. to define the Immaculate Conception in order to stop the wrangling, the Popes replying that the doctrine was not definable as not being in Scripture?

The Popes have **never** given such a decision. Paul V in 1617 forbade anyone to teach **publicly** that Mary was not immaculate. Gregory V. in 1622 ordered the discussion to stop until the Church should have given an **official decision.** Alexander VII said that the Immaculate Conception of Mary was the **common doctrine** of the Church and that no one must deny it. None of these Popes gave a dogmatic definition, but rather a **disciplinary** ruling. Pope Pius IX. defined the doctrine finally in 1854.

18. Why call Mary a virgin? Seeing that she was a mother. The linking of the two terms is an insult to reason.

The assertion that an omnipotent God is limited by the **natural** laws, which He Himself established, is an insult to reason. Jesus, the child of Mary, was conceived **miraculously** without the intervention of any human father, and was born miraculously, Mary's virginity being preserved throughout. I do not claim that any natural laws were responsible for this event. I claim that God was responsible, and the only way you can show that the doctrine is not reasonable is by proving that there is no God, or that He could not do what Catholic doctrine asserts.

19. Where does it say in Scripture that Mary was ever a virgin?

Isaiah the prophet (VII., 14) certainly predicted a supernatural and extraordinary birth of the Messiah when he wrote, "The Lord Himself shall give you a sign. Behold a virgin shall conceive and bear a son; and his name shall be called Emmanuel." St. Luke says, "The angel Gabriel was sent from God . . . to a virgin . . . and the virgin's name was Mary." When Mary was offered the dignity of becoming the mother of the Messiah, a privilege to which any Jewish maiden would ordinarily look forward with eager desire, she urged against the prospect the fact that she had no intention of motherhood. "How shall this be done, because **I know not man.**" She does not refer to the past, but by using the present tense indicates her present and persevering intention. The angel assured her that her child would be due to the miraculous operation of the Holy Spirit, and that she would not be asked to forfeit the virginity she prized so highly, and then only did she consent. Luke I., 26-38. When Jesus was born, Mary had none of the suffering usually associated with childbirth. The child was born miraculously. Mary herself in no way incapacitated. She herself **attended** to her **own** needs and those of the child. "She brought forth her first-born son, and wrapped him up in swaddling clothes, and laid him in a manger." Lk. II., 7. The Virgin Birth means that Mary had at one and the same time the privilege of **Motherhood** and the privilege of **Maidenhood.**

20. Did not Mary, to cloak her own sin, persuade St. Joseph that her child was of the Holy Ghost?

No. That is absolutely false. Mary, saluted by an angel as **full of grace,** was the **purest** and **holiest** woman who ever lived on this earth. And, as a matter of fact, with sublime confidence in God, Mary refrained from explaining the event to St. Joseph, leaving all to God. As St. Matthew Mt. I, 20, tells us, "Behold the angel of the Lord appeared to him in his sleep, saying, 'Joseph, son of David, fear not to take unto thee Mary thy wife, for that which is conceived in her is of the Holy Ghost.'" What you suggest has been said by certain people merely because the

Catholic Church **honors** Mary. Their hatred of the Catholic Church is so great that they dislike all she loves, and are willing to overlook any injury to Christ in fostering their hatred. Yet how can they hope to please Christ by **dishonoring** His mother? Every true child bitterly resents disrespect to his mother, and Christ was the best son who ever lived. The more we honor Mary the more we honor Christ, for the honor we show her is because of Christ. If He were not the central figure, Mary would have been forgotten long ago.

21. If Jesus was born of a virgin why does he say nothing about it?

We do not know that He said **nothing** about it. The evangelists do not record any **special** utterances of Christ on this subject, but they do not pretend to record **all** that He ever said. St. Luke tells us that when He met the two disciples on the way to Emmaus, "beginning at Moses and all the prophets, He expounded to them in all the Scriptures, the things that were concerning him." XXIV., 27. There is every probability that He explained His advent into this world according to the prophecy of Isaiah. Meantime the Gospels do record the fact that Mary **was a virgin,** and their words are as reliable in this as when they record the utterances of Christ.

22. To prove Davidic descent both Matthew and Luke give the genealogy of Joseph, useless were not Joseph the Father of Christ.

The genealogy of Joseph was that of Mary also. They were kinspeople of the same Davidic stock. The Jews as a rule counted their generations only in the **male** line, and such a generation alone would appeal to the Jews for whom Matthew above all wrote. The same St. Matthew records that the angel told Joseph that the child was conceived miraculously by the Holy Ghost and not through the intervention of man. St. Luke in turn left no doubt as to his mind on the subject when he carefully wrote that "Jesus Himself was beginning about the age of thirty years; being (as it was supposed) the son of Joseph." III., 23.

23. St. Matthew says that Joseph knew her not till she brought forth her first-born son. I., 25.

Nor did he. And the expression "till" in Hebrew usage has no necessary reference to the future. Thus in Gen. VIII., 7, we read that "the dove went forth from the ark and did not return **till** the waters dried up." That expression does not suggest that it returned then. It did not return at all, having found resting places. Nor does the expression first-born child imply that there were other children afterwards.

Thus Exodus says, "Every first-born shall be sanctified unto God." Parents had not to wait to see if other children were born before they could call the first their first-born!

24. Matt. XIII, 55-56, says, "His brethren James and Joseph, and Simon and Jude: and his sisters, are they not all with us?"

The Jewish expression "brothers and sisters of the Lord" in Scripture merely refers to **relationship** in the same tribe or stock. Cousins often came under that title. In all nations the word brother has a wide significance, as when one Mason will call another a brother Mason without suggesting that he was born of the same mother. The same St. Matthew speaks explicitly of "Mary, the mother of James and Joseph" in XXVII., 56, obviously alluding to a Mary who was not the mother of Jesus but who was married to Cleophas, the brother of Joseph.

25. There would not be two girls in the one family called Mary.

There certainly could be. And St. John XIX., 25, writes that there stood by the cross of Jesus "His mother, and His mother's sister, Mary of Cleophas." But even here, Mary of Cleophas need not have been a sister in the first degree of blood-relationship, but rather of the same lineage in more remote degrees of either consanguinity or affinity.

26. Why are Protestants, who believe in Scripture, so convinced that Mary had other children?

They are not inspired by love for Christ, or for the mother of Christ, or for Scripture in their doctrine. Their main desire is to maintain a doctrine **differing** from that of the Catholic Church. But it is a position which is rapidly going **out of fashion.** Learned Protestant scholars today deny as emphatically as any Catholic that Mary had other children. When Our Lord, dying on the cross, commended His mother to the care of St. John, He did so precisely because He was **her only child,** and He knew that Mary had no other children to care for her. The idea that Mary had other children is **disrespectful** to the Holy Spirit who claimed and sanctified her as His sanctuary. It insults Christ, who was the only-begotten of His mother even as He was the only-begotten of His Heavenly Father. It insults Mary, who would have been guilty of a great **ingratitude** to God, if she threw away the gift of virginity which God had so carefully preserved for her in the conception of Christ. It insults St. Joseph. God had told him by an angel to take Mary to wife, and that the child to be born of her had **no earthly father** but was the very Son of God. God merely gave St. Joseph the **privilege** of protecting her good name amongst the undiscerning Jews, and He chose a God-fearing man who would respect her. Knowing that her child was God Himself in human form, Joseph would at once regard her as on a plane **far superior** to that of any ordinary human being, and to him, as to us, the mere thought of her becoming a mother to merely earthly children would have seemed a sacrilege.

27. You urge these privileges granted to Mary as the foundation of your devotion to her, yet Christ said, "Rather blessed are they who hear the word of God and keep it." Luke XI, 28.

Would you presume to say that Mary, whom the angel addressed as full of grace, did not hear the Word of God and keep it? You have missed the sense of the passage to which you allude. In Luke XI., 27, a woman praised the one who had the honor to be the mother of Christ. Christ did not for a moment deny it, as you would like to believe. The sense of His words is simple, "Yes, she is blessed. But better to hear God's word and keep it, thus attain holiness, than to be My mother. You cannot all imitate Mary by being My mother; but you can do so by **hearing** God's word and **keeping** it." The thought that those who hear God's word and keep it are rather blessed than Mary because she did not is simply **absurd.** "Henceforth," declared Mary prophetically, "all generations shall call me blessed." Lk. I., 48. And Elizabeth saluted her with the words, "Blessed art thou among women." Lk. I., 42.

28. How do you prove Mary's bodily assumption into Heaven?

No Christian could dispute the fact that Mary's soul is in Heaven. Christ certainly did not suffer the soul of His own mother to be lost. The doctrine of her bodily assumption after her death is not contained in Scripture, but is guaranteed by **tradition** and by the **teaching** of the Catholic Church. That Scripture omits to record the fact is **no argument** against it. Omission is not denial. Meantime, early traditions positively record the fact, and negatively we note that, whilst the mortal remains of a St. Peter and of a St. Paul are jealously possessed and honored in Rome, no city or Christian center has ever claimed to possess the mortal remains of Our Lady. Certainly relics of Our Lady would be regarded as having greater value than those of any Saint or Apostle, so nearly was she related to Christ. And it was **most fitting** that the body of Mary, who had been preserved even from the taint of original sin, should not have been allowed to corrupt. After all, it was just as easy for God to take her glorified body to Heaven **at once** as it will be to take the glorified bodies of all the saved at the last day. However, the definite sanction of this doctrine by the Catholic Church is sufficient assurance of the fact.

29. I have discovered 27 virgin-born Saviors in my studies of mythology.

You would find it very difficult to **name** them. However, granting that you have read of some such claims, a little further study would show you that a critical and comparative examination such as Christian doctrine has had to undergo, leaves these mythological claims devoid of reality, whilst the Christian fact emerges unscathed.

30. At evening devotions in a Catholic Church I heard many prayers to Mary. I cannot find in Scripture where Mary is to be worshipped in the same way as Christ.

I am not surprised, for such a doctrine is nowhere taught in Scripture. Moreover if any Catholic dared to worship Mary in the same way as he worships Christ, he would be guilty of a most serious sin, and no Catholic priest could give him absolution unless he promised never to do so again. But that does not mean that one must **deprive** Mary of all honor.

31. St. Bonaventure said, "Into thy hands, O Lady, I commend my spirit." Thus he served the creature more than the creator to whom alone such words should be addressed.

St. Bonaventure did not serve the creature more than the Creator. In commending his soul to Mary he was not commending it to anyone opposed to God. He did is because of God, who chose Mary as the second Eve. Eve brought us forth to misery and to death; Mary brought us forth to happiness and to life when she brought forth our Saviour. Like the kings from the East, St. Bonaventure knew that after the long journey through this life, he would also find the child Jesus with Mary, His mother, and that if he commended his soul to the mother he would necessarily find himself in the presence of the child, even in eternity. Gladly on my own deathbed would I utter the words used by St. Bonaventure. As Jesus came to us through Mary, so we shall go to Him through her, whether we think of it or not.

32. Mary is no different from your own mother.

As the street Arab replied to a similar objection. "But there's an immense difference between the sons. My mother is the mother of me. Mary is the mother of God."

33. You speak as if Jesus looks on His mother just as you look on your mother.

As surely as my mother is my mother, He knows that His mother is His mother; and He treats her as such.

34. Jesus was a good son but he recognized only one being, the omnipotent God.

Had he ignored Mary He would not have been a very good son, nor would He have had much respect for God who said, "Honor thy father and thy mother." Christ was a perfect example of virtue in all things. And if He did not recognize Mary, why did He go down to Nazareth and be **subject** to her? Why did he perform His first miracle at her **request**? And why did He make such special **provision** for her at the moment of His death?

35. When someone praised Mary, Christ paid no attention, but said that only those are blessed who keep the word of God. Lk. XI., 28.

The Gospels are fragmentary accounts, and we do not know all that transpired on that occasion. But even so, the actual text is not opposed in any way to the honor we give to Mary. Someone praised Mary. Christ replied, "Yea, rather blessed are they who hear the word of God and keep it." Not for a moment did He intend to deny that Mary had done this. He practically says, "Yes. She is blest in being my mother. But it is a greater blessing to serve God." And, from one point of view, the fidelity with which Mary undoubtedly served God was a greater blessing to her than merely being the mother of Christ. Any idea that Christ, the best of sons, was trying to belittle His mother is absurd. And if you have such faith in Scripture, what do you do as regards the prophecy of Mary in Lk. I., 48? "From henceforth," she predicted, "all generations shall call me blessed." Yet blessed are they who hear the word of God and keep it! We Catholics call Mary blessed indeed, whilst many Protestants search Scripture in the fond hope of proving something to her discredit!

36. Christ called her, "Woman," when he said, "Woman, behold thy son." John XIX, 26.

In the language Christ spoke, that word was a term of **great respect** however harshly it may sound in our modern English language. Our Lord would have been the last to slight His mother, a thing we despise in every man; and above all in His last and most tender words to her. Nor are we likely to please Him by seeking to dishonor her.

37. Did He not say to her at the marriage feast of Cana, "Woman, what is that to thee and to Me?" John II, 4.

He did. But most certainly He intended no reproach to Mary. Her action was one of pure charity to others. Foreseeing the possible distress of others, she asked Him to relieve them; and He would not rebuke so unselfish a thought. Nor would He speak to her with any trace of disrespect. Then, too, had Mary asked a wrong thing, Christ would not have done it, nor would He have sanctioned a request He had to rebuke. And Mary knew that she had not been reprehended, or she would not have told the waiters to do what her Son would tell them. She would have dropped the matter. Why, then, did Christ speak thus? It was His first miracle, the first public sign of His divinity wrought by Himself. And He wanted to bring out publicly the fact that He was doing it, not as the son of an earthly mother and according to His human nature, but calling upon His divine nature as the eternal Son of God. He did it because His mother requested it, but He did not do it by any power derived from His mother. He thus brought out both for the listeners and for us that this beginning of miracles was proof of His divinity, although in appearance He seemed but man.

38. Why do you call Mary Queen of Heaven?

Because Mary is undoubtedly in Heaven, and Jesus is King of Heaven. Since Jesus is "King of kings and Lord of lords," it is certain that Mary His mother rejoices in queenly dignity.

39. Why pray to Mary at all?

Because God wills that we should do so, and because such prayers to her are of the **utmost value.** God often wills to give certain favors only on condition that we go to some **secondary** agent. Sodom was to be spared through the **intercession** of Abraham; Gen. XVIII, 20-33. Naaman, the leper, was to be cured only through the **waters** of the Jordan, 4 Kings V, 9-14. Now Mary is, and must ever remain, the Mother of Christ. She still has a mother's rights and privileges, and is able to obtain for us many graces. But let us view things reasonably. If I desire to pray, I can certainly pray to God **directly.** Yet would you blame me if, at times, I were to ask **my own** earthly mother to pray for me also? Such a request is really a prayer to her that she may intercede for me with God. Certainly, if I met the mother of Christ on earth, I would ask her to pray for me, and she would do so. And in her more perfect state with

Christ in Heaven she is **more able** to help me.

40. But a prayer to God directly must be more efficacious than a prayer to Mary.

Not necessarily. It might well be that God intends to honor Our Lady by granting the favor I seek through her intercession in a particular way. In that case the grace is to be given through her provided I honor her by addressing myself to her. Again, every prayer to Mary is in reality the asking of a favor also. It is often better to ask God for a favor and to have someone else praying to God with one for the same favor. Two prayers are better than one. And above all, when the other one praying is Christ's own mother.

41. God loves you more than Mary loves you.

That is so. But He loves Mary more than He loves me. And as she is more pleasing to God than I am, He will be more ready to grant her requests.

42. It is unscriptural to attribute power to Mary.

That is a very **unscriptural** statement. At His mother's request Jesus changed water into wine at Cana, though He had said, "My time is not yet come." John II, 4. St. James tells us that "the prayer of a just man availeth much." Ja. V, 16. How much more the prayer of Mary!

43. Does the Bible sanction such prayers to Mary?

Yes. All through the Bible you will find God conferring favors through the **prayers of others.** In the Old Testament we read of the prayers of Abraham, Moses, and of the various prophets. In the New Testament, St. James V, 16, tells us to "pray for one another," in the text I have just quoted. If we must always pray directly to God and may not ask the prayers of others why did St. Paul write to the Thessalonians, "Pray for us that we may be delivered from importunate and evil men"? 2 Thess. III, 2. Why did he not ask directly of God, instead of asking the prayers of the Thessalonians? Or would you be **more** scriptural than the New Testament itself?

44. There is but one mediator; there is no place for Mary.

Christ is the **principal** mediator in His own right, Mary is a **secondary** mediatrix, through, with, and in Christ. Without Him she would have no power, and therefore He is the source of all mediation with God on behalf of men.

45. How can you blend the mediation of others with that of Christ?

It follows from the doctrine of the Communion of Saints. Remember that, by Baptism, every Christian is incorporated with Christ. St. Paul says, "Christ is the head; ye are the members." I Cor. XI, 3 XII, 27. So close is this union that Christ says, "Whoever gives you to drink a cup of water in my name because you belong to Christ; amen, I say to you, he shall not lose his reward." Mk. IX, 40. Every Christian is Christ in a most intimate way. St. Paul tells us that if a baptized person sins, he takes the members of Christ and makes them the members of inquity! When that same St. Paul was persecuting the Christians before his conversion, Christ appeared to him and said, "Saul, Saul, why persecutest Thou Me?" Acts IX, 4. He did not say, "Why persecutest thou My disciples?" He could equally say, when we pray to Mary or to the saints, "What asketh thou of Me?" When we honor Our Lady or the saints, we honor, not their own merely human and created nature, but we honor Christ in them according to the doctrines of Scripture. The Catholic Church is the only **completely scriptural** Church.

46. Do Catholics believe that Mary is omnipotent?

No. God alone is omnipotent. But through Mary we have access to the omnipotence of God.

47. How do you know that Mary hears you?

The Catholic Church guarantees that, and she is here to tell us the **truth** about such things in the name of Christ and with His authority. Reason also assures us that, as she could know our prayers in this life and pray for us in turn, so she can do so in the more perfect state in Heaven. Finally, experience proves it, for she has manifested her power in thousands of concrete instances in answer to prayer.

48. Why should Mary be recognized as being greater than any other woman?

She was picked out by God to be the sacred repository of God's own Son, to furnish, so to speak, the human texture, flesh, and blood from which was to be woven the garb of divinity. If before birth we could have the **privilege of choosing** our own natural mother, and if we ever had the power of making that mother whatever we chose, would we ever make her short of anything but the loveliest lady in the world, or would we ever have endowed her with those qualities which would make us apologize to men either for moral blemishes or physical weaknesses? No. I think we would give to her the qualities and virtues which would make all men love her eternally. If you and I then, with our natural natures would have done all this to the woman who gave us life, who meant so much to us, should we not suppose that God would do the same and more for the Mother of His Son? This he did do. He arrayed her in the peerless jewel of Divine Grace, a grace that was higher than any grace given to any saint, angel, or archangel. Angels were created to serve God. Mary was created to be the Mother, the shrine, the tabernacle of God-made Man. Mary is to be honored above all women as the prophecies of the Old Testament declare, precisely because of the **royal role** she plays as Co-Redemptrix with Christ in the Divine Redemption.

49. I don't see the necessity of hailing her as the Co-Redemptrix with Christ.

See then what is happening to the non-Catholic world for denying that role of Mary. In Catholicism, they tell us, there is **too much** emphasis and the **wrong** emphasis on the Mother of Jesus. If we ever begin a religion by **eliminating** the Mother, we shall eventually wind up by **eliminating** the Son. Thus when the Reformers did away with the Mother, they paved the way for doing away with the Son. If we get rid of the one, we will soon get rid of the other. Germany began by putting the Mother in the tomb of oblivion or on the dusty pages of history and after four hundred years Germany is now trying to get rid of the Son. If we can judge correctly the attitude of the American Federation of Churches, our Blessed Savior is being rapidly brought down to the mere status of a man. We can reasonably be suspicious that religions that have taken Mary out, have slurred this wonderful Lady, and when we insult the Mother we insult the Son. We can never have a Son without a Mother in the natural order of things; in the Divine order of things we can never have a Christ without a Mary. If we smash her statues and white-wash Our Lady's Chapel or chisel the Child from the Mother, we run the risk of smashing the entire statue of Christianity, for those two holy heads of Jesus and Mary are too close together for their halos not to mingle and to cross.

50. Attending a Catholic Church one evening I was disgusted by the rigmarole called the Rosary. What is the Rosary?

The Rosary is a special form of **devotion to Mary**. One takes a set of beads, divided into five sections, each section consisting of one large bead and ten small beads. Holding the large bead, one says the Our Father, and on each of the small ones, the Hail Mary. Between each section or decade the Gloria is said. Whilst saying the prayers, one meditates or thinks of the joys, or sorrows, or glories of

Christ's life and of that of His Mother. It is a very beautiful form of prayer with which you were disgusted merely because you did not understand it. The Rosary is a Bible for the **Blind** and the **unlearned.** In the so-called Dark Ages which were indeed the Ages of Faith, the Church taught the great masses, who could not read, the mysteries of the Bible through the meditations of the Rosary.

51. The Rosary is a relic of the superstitious Middle Ages, when it was meant for ignorant people.

The use of beads dates from the earliest centuries. The prayers embodied in the Rosary were composed by Christ Himself in the case of the Our Father and by the Angel Gabriel, St. Elizabeth, and the Council of Ephesus in the 5th century, in the case of the Hail Mary. We are in very good company with those prayers. As a devotion, with its loving contemplation of the mysteries of the life, death and resurrection of Our Lord it appeals to rich and poor, to learned and ignorant alike, as Christianity itself was meant to do.

52. When were beads invented, and what do they symbolize?

It is impossible to say when beads were first used. As an aid to memory, the early Christians used to put a number of pebbles in one pocket, transferring them to another as they said each prayer, so that they could be sure of completing such prayers each day as their devotion inspired. Later, berries or pebbles were strung together for the purpose. In the Middle Ages sections of these beads were adapted to the different meditations which compose the Rosary, the sections being a numerical help to meditate for a given period of time upon each allotted subject. The symbolism is expressed in the word Rosary. A Rosary is a garland of flowers. One rose does not make a Rosary. Prayers are the flowers of the spiritual life, and in offering that group of prayers, known as the Rosary, we lay a garland of spiritual flowers at the feet of God.

53. Christ did not have a Crucifix or Rosary beads.

He made the first Crucifix. That He did not use Rosary beads does not affect the question. He never had a **copy** of the New Testament in His hands, yet you do not **reject** the New Testament because of that!

54. Between each Our Father to God, it throws in ten prayers to Mary!

You've got it the wrong way 'round. Between each ten Hail Marys an Our Father is said. The Rosary is essentially a devotion to Mary, honoring her whom God Himself so honored. And it honors her particularly in her relation to Christ, whose life is the subject of the meditations. The Our Father abstracts from the Incarnation of Christ; the Hail Mary is full of reverence to Our Lord in His birth into this world for us.

55. Would not the Rosary be just as efficient if said with one Our Father, one Hail Mary, and one Gloria?

It would not be the Rosary then, but some other type of devotion. Nor would such a devotion be as efficient, for meditation whilst saying ten Hail Marys is better than meditation whilst saying one. But your trouble seems to be based on the mere question of number. That is quite immaterial.

56. It is not. Christ said, "Use not vain repetitions as do the heathen, who think in their much speaking to be heard." St. Mt. VI., 7.

Vain repetition in the manner of heathens is forbidden, but not **useful** repetition which is not in the manner of heathens. Vain repetition relies mechanically upon the mere number of prayers or formulas uttered. But Catholics do not rely on the mere repetition of prayers, nor upon their multiplication, but on the **intrinsic worth** of each prayer and upon the fervor and earnestness with which it is said. Two prayers said well, one immediately after the other, are as good as the same two prayers said well with twenty-four hours between them. Time is nothing to God, in whose sight 1,000 years are but as a day. He does not mind whether there be two seconds between our prayers or two years; the prayers themselves are just as pleasing to Him. If you take the principle behind your objection, and push it to its full conclusion, you could say the Our Father but once in your life. If you said it once each year, it would be repetition. How often may you say it? Once a month? Once a week? Once a day? If daily, what would be wrong with saying it hourly? If you have just concluded one Our Father, why may you not begin it again at once? Does it suddenly become an evil prayer?

Your Bible has a faulty translation of these words, "Use not vain repetitions as the heathens do." The Greek verb "battologein" of the original does not mean such a thing at all. The Douay version translates correctly when it says, **"speak not much."** St. Mt. wanted **action** and less **talk.**

57. If repetition adds to effectiveness, why stop at ten Hail Marys? Why not more?

It is the nature of this devotion that the Rosary should

be composed of decades, or groups of ten. It would not be the Rosary otherwise. Repetition certainly adds to effectiveness, if the prayers are said well. Just before His passion, Christ prayed "the **third time,** saying the self-same word." Mt. XXVI., 44. He thought it good to say the same prayer three times in succession. Why did He limit it to three times? If good to say it three times, why not twenty times? He thought three sufficient for His purpose. So, too, we consider the period taken by the recital of ten Hail Marys sufficient time for the amount of reflection we desire to give to each mystery of the Rosary.

58. Does not Scripture advise short prayer rather than long rosaries?

No. Long hypocritical prayers are condemned. Prayer may be prolonged, but it must not be hypocritical, mechanical, or insincere. Christ spoke a parable to them that, "We ought always to pray, and not to faint." Lk. XVIII, 1. He Himself "went out into a mountain to pray, and He passed the whole night in prayer to God." Lk. VI., 12. "We cease not to pray for you," wrote St. Paul to the Colossians I, 9. "Night and day we more abundantly pray for you," he wrote to the Thessalonians I, 3, 10.

59. Anyway short mental prayers must be better than long distracted prayers.

Short fervent interior prayers are better than long distracted vocal prayers. But, given equally fervent prayers said with due attention, long ones are better than short ones. It is certainly better to give more time to prayer than less! And if distractions do present themselves, it is better to give up the distractions than to give up the prayers. Mental prayer is good, but vocal prayer is equally good if said well, and sometimes better. Thus Christ taught the Apostles a vocal prayer called the Our Father. So well did they learn it by heart that they were able to write it down years later word for word.

60. Why do you omit from the Our Father the words "For Thine is the Kingdom, the Power, and the Glory forever and ever"?

Because Our Lord did not add those words to the prayer as He taught it. There is nothing wrong with the words in themselves. In fact, they are very beautiful. But they are not Sacred Scripture. Some early Catholic copyist wrote those words in a margin; later copyist mistakenly transcribed them into the text; and the Protestant translators made use of a copy of the New Testament with the words thus included. All scholars today admit the words to be an interpolation. We Catholics do not use them.

61. Why do Catholic Churches ring bells at daybreak, noon, and sunset?

The ringing of these bells is to remind Catholics to say the Angelus, a short devotion in honor of the incarnation of Christ. Three rings are given three times separately, and then nine rings, according to an ancient custom. The devotion is called the Angelus because the first words of the prayers to be said begin as follows: "The Angel of the Lord declared unto Mary." The Angelus, therefore, reminds us of the message of the Angel Gabriel who brought the good news of the birth of Jesus Christ. And Catholics are asked to begin the day by remembering this great benefit; to recollect it again at noon, and at sunset or the close of the day. An old English manuscript, written of course in England's Catholic days before the Reformation, says that the Angelus in the morning should remind us of Christ's resurrection at dawn; at noon of His death on the cross; and at eventide of His birth at midnight in the cave in Bethlehem. In any case, the Angelus is to remind Catholics of the fact that the Son of God came into this world for the redemption of mankind, and that they themselves should never forget it.

62. What do the three threes, and the nine bells signify?

The origin of the number of bells to be tolled is uncertain. The triple ringing reminds us of the Most Holy Trinity. The final nine bells may have been arranged merely for the sake of harmony and symmetry, although some writers see in that number a reminder of the nine choirs of Angels who invite us to adore God with them.

63. Why pray to Saints? Is it not better to pray to God direct?

Not always. The same answer applies here as in the case of prayers to the Virgin Mary, who after all is the greatest of the Saints. God may wish to give certain favors through the intercession of some given Saint. In such a case, it is better to seek the intercession of that Saint as God wishes. I can decide to give you a gift myself, or to do so through a friend. In the latter case you do me greater honor by accepting it from my friend than by refusing my way of giving it to you, and insolently demanding it directly from myself in person.

64. I pray that you may see the futility of praying to Saints who can do nothing for you. Christ is the only Mediator.

By your very prayer you are attempting to mediate between God and myself on my behalf. I do not criticize the principle of praying for others. I believe in that. But I do criticize your praying for me in violation of your own principles. If the Saints cannot be mediators by praying for me, nor can you. Your prayers would be futile; they could do nothing for me; and you would be wasting your time.

65. When did God tell anyone to pray to human beings?
When the Catholic Church teaches us that prayer to the Saints is right and useful, it is God teaching us that truth through His Church. But the doctrine is clearly enough indicated in Scripture also. I have mentioned Abraham's prayer for Sodom. Gen. XVIII, 20. The Jews asked Moses to go to speak to God on their behalf. God Himself said to Eliphaz, the Themanite, "My wrath is kindled against thee . . . . but my servant Job shall pray for you. His face I will accept that folly be not imputed to you." Job XLII, 8. Earlier in that same book we read, "Call now if there will be any that will answer thee, and turn to some of the Saints." V., 1. His enemies meant that Job was too wicked to be heard, but they knew that it was lawful to invoke the Saints. Long after the death of Jeremiah, Onias said of that prophet, "This is the lover of his brethren and of the people of Israel. This is he that prayeth much for the people and for all the holy city; Jeremiah, the prophet of God." 2 Mach. XV., 14. St. James says that "prayer of a just man availeth much." V, 16. If his prayer is valuable, it is worth while to ask his prayers. If you say, "Yes. That is all right whilst a man is still in this life and on earth," I ask whether you think he has less power when in Heaven with God? In Rev. VIII., 4, St. John says that he saw "the prayers of the Saints ascending up before God from the hand of an angel." If I can ask my own mother to pray for me whilst she is still in this life, surely I can do so when she is with God! She does not know less when she rejoices in the Vision of God; she has not less interest in me; and she is not less charitably disposed towards me then. We Catholics believe in the Communion of Saints, and are in communion with them. But for you the doctrine of the Apostles' Creed, "I believe in the Communion of Saints," must be a meaningless formula. Christ is not particularly honored by our ignoring those who loved and served Him best, and whom He loves so much.

66. The Lord's Prayer shows that God Himself hears our prayers.

Correct. And He hears the prayers we address to the Saints, and their prayers also on our behalf. And those prayers, added to our own, give us additional claims to be heard by God in a favorable way.

67. By what authority does the Catholic Church make Saints?

The decree of canonization does not make a Saint. It simply declares infallibly that a given person has lived such a holy life with the help of God's grace that he is a Saint. When someone like a Francis of Assisi lives such a holy life that all people are compelled to admire it, the Church is often asked to say whether such a person is worthy to be honored publicly as a Saint. The Church then carefully collects all possible information, and, after due consideration, says yes or no. If the Church says yes, the name of the person to be venerated is put into the Canon or catalogue of those who have become Saints by their heroic lives of virtue. The Church has the authority of Christ for these decisions, for He sent her with His authority to teach all nations in matters of faith and morals, and she could not tell us officially that a given person was a perfect model of Christian virtue if such a person were not.

68. Who has the final say as to whether a soul deserves canonization?

The Pope. Before he defines that a given soul is indeed a Saint, the advocates of the cause must prove that the person in question exercised all Christian virtue in a heroic degree—supreme faith, hope, and charity; perfect prudence, justice, fortitude, and temperance. Also God's own testimony by proven miracles wrought through the person's intercession is required. The infallibility of the Church in such decisions is, as I have said, but an application of ordinary infallibility in matters of faith and morals, in so far as the Church could not err in proposing a given life as an exemplification of perfect Christian virtue.

69. How does the Church know that those she calls Saints are in Heaven?

With the assistance of the Holy Spirit, she can and does know. She knows God, and knows what holiness is. She examines the life of the holy person, and says that such a life certainly could not lead a soul to Hell. The Church canonizes only those whose heroic virtue has been proved. And perfect charity before death destroys all sin, and all punishment due to sin. There is no place where such a soul could be, save in Heaven. Also miracles wrought by God in honor of such a one are His guarantee.

70. Why does the Church allot different duties to different Saints?

She does not. She asks the special protection and intercession of certain Saints in special circumstances; and this is based upon what we know of their particular interest whilst they were on earth, or upon favors obtained already through their intercession since their death.

71. Why do Catholics worship relics of Saints?

They do not worship relics as they worship God, by adoration. If you mean worship in the sense of honor or veneration, then Catholics certainly venerate the relics of Saints. The law, "Honor thy father and thy mother," extends to their persons, body and soul; to their reputations, and to all connected with them. We reverence their remains even after death. And if we are not to venerate the remains and relics of the Saints who have been so entirely consecrated to God, are we to desecrate them? Or are we to be blandly indifferent to them as to the bleached bones of some dead animal lying in the fields? The Catholic doctrine, forbidding adoration, yet commanding respect and veneration, is the only possible Christian conduct.

72. I don't object to that kind of veneration. I object to the expecting of favors through relics.

No real difficulty arises in this matter. No one holds that material relics of themselves possess any innate talismanic value. But God Himself can certainly grant favors even of a temporal nature through the relics of Saints, thus honoring His Saints, and rewarding the faith and piety of some given Catholic. St. Matthew tells us that the diseased came to Christ. "And they besought Him that they might touch but the hem of His garment. And as many as touched were made whole." Matt. XIV., 36. Again we read of a woman who touched the hem of Christ's garment and who was cured. "And Jesus, knowing in Himself the virtue that had proceeded from Him, said: "Who has touched my garments." Mk. V., 30. You may reply that these incidents concerned Christ, and that, whilst He was still living in this world. But that does not affect the principle that God can grant temporal favors through inanimate things. And if you look up 2 Kings, XIII., 21, in your own Protestant version of the Bible, you will find that a dead man, who was being buried in the sepulchre of Elisha, was restored to life the moment his body came into contact with the bones of that great prophet of God. In the Acts of the Apostles, too, we read of a most **Catholic,** and most **un-Protestant** procedure. "God wrought by the hand of Paul more than common miracles. So that even there were brought from his body to the sick, **handkerchiefs** and **aprons,** and the diseases departed from them." Acts XIX, 11-12. But you will notice that it was **God** who wrought these miracles. And we Catholics say that God can quite easily do **similar things** even in our own days. As a matter of historical fact, He has wrought such things throughout the course of the ages **within** the Catholic Church.

73. Are not relics received and venerated without a particle of proof that they are genuine?

No. The Catholic Church is very prudent in this matter, and her law declares that those relics alone may be publicly venerated which have **authentic documents** accompanying them, and proving them to be genuine. These documents can be given only by one authorized by the Holy See to grant them. If the documents be lost, no relic may be offered for public veneration by the faithful without a special decree from a Bishop who can guarantee the relic as genuine. But even should a Catholic venerate as a relic some object which is not authentic, such veneration is at least well meant, and directed towards the one whom the object is believed to represent.

74. Why are Catholic Churches decorated with images and statues, in direct violation of the Second Commandment?

The Second Commandment is, "Thou shalt not take the name of the Lord thy God in vain." Protestants, of course, call that the Third Commandment. But they are wrong in doing so, having taken that part of the first commandment which refers to images as the second of God's commandments. But do those words forbid the **making** of images? They do not. God was forbidding idolatry, not the making of images. He said, "Thou shalt not make to thyself any graven image of anything in the Heaven above, or in the earth beneath. Thou shalt not **bow down** to them nor **worship** them." God deliberately adds those last words, yet you ignore them. He forbids men to make images in order to **adore** them. But He does not forbid the making of images. You will find the commandments given in Exodus, XX. But in that same Book, XXV., 18, you will find God ordering the Jews to make images of Angels! Would you accuse God of not knowing the **sense** of His own law? He says, "Thou shalt make also two **cherubims** of beaten gold, on the two sides of the oracle." In other words, the Jews were to make images of things in the Heaven above. And if your interpretation be true, why do you violate God's law by making images of things in the earth beneath? Why images of generals and **politicians** in our parks? Why photographs of friends and relatives? On your theory you could not even take a snapshot of a gum tree. You would be making an image of a thing in the earth beneath. You strain at a gnat and swallow a camel! This is the **fruit** of your private interpretation of Scripture. No. God does not forbid the making of images; He forbids the making of images in order to adore them.

75. I have seen more idols in Catholic Churches than sincere Christians.

You have never seen an **idol** in a Catholic Church. An image is an idol only when it is the **object** of divine worship. You have seen images in Catholic Churches, but every Catholic knows that divine worship cannot be offered to such images. Would you call the Statue of Liberty in New York harbor, an idol? As for your not seeing sincere Christians in a Catholic Church, you cannot expect to test the sincerity of a Christian by the color of his tie or the shape of his shoes. Are not the stained glass windows in your churches **images?** Are they idols for you? You may not like images of Christ on a Cross, but you make no bones about **singing** in your hymns "in the **Cross of Christ** we glory." Is there sense in your singing about the Cross and then rebelling against a real cross?

76. God forbade us to worship plaster statues as Catholics do; yet you send missionaries to convert heathens who do the same thing.

God absolutely forbids us to worship wooden and stone statues, and Catholics are not so foolish as to commit so serious a sin. But Catholics do honor representations of those who are in Heaven, just as we all honor our dead soldiers by tributes of respect to the Cenotaph. If I lift my hat to the flag of my country as I pass the memorial to our dead soldiers, am I honoring the cloth or the stone, or what it **stands for?** If it be lawful in that case, it is certainly lawful to honor the memorials of the **dead heroes** of Christianity, the Saints. Our missionaries go to heathen tribes to save them from the idolatrous worship of man-made gods.

77. I have seen Catholics on their knees adoring and praying to statues in their churches.

You have not. You have seen Catholics kneeling at prayer, and perhaps kneeling before an image of Christ, or of Our Lady. But if you concluded that they were **praying to the statues** that was not the fault of the Catholics. It was your own fault in so far as you judged them according to your own preconceived ideas. Without bothering to ask for information, you guessed and guessed wrongly. Before an image of Mary, Catholics may go on their knees and pray to God through the intercession of that Mother of Christ whom the statue represents. But you have **no right** to accuse them of praying to the statue. Were you to kneel down by your bedside at night for a last prayer, could you be regarded as **adoring** or **praying** to **your mattress?**

78. But I have seen a Catholic kiss the feet of a statue of Christ.

If I kiss the **photograph** of my mother, am I honoring a piece of cardboard? Or is it a tribute of love and respect offered to my mother? A Catholic reverences images and statues only in so far as they **remind** him of God, of Christ, or of Our Lady and the Saints. Where a pagan adores and worships a thing of wood **in itself,** I kiss the cross, not because it is a piece of wood, but because it **stands for** Christ and for His sufferings on my behalf. And I am sure that Our Lord looks down from Heaven and says, "Bless the child; he at least appreciates My love for him." Your mistake is that you try to judge interior dispositions from exterior conduct—a dangerous policy always.

79. Catholics raise their hats when passing a church; why not when passing statues in a Catholic store window?

The Catholic who raises his hat when passing a Catholic Church does so as an act of reverence for the Presence of Christ in the Holy Eucharist. But Christ is not thus present in stores selling Catholic articles of devotion. But of course you missed the point, and took it for granted that Catholic men lift their hats because statues are present in the Church. Then you concluded that they ought to do so when they see statues in a store window.

80. If the use of statues is all right, why did the Catholic Church cut out the Second Commandment?

You are asking an impossible question. You might as well ask me, "Why has China declared war on Afghanistan?" No man could answer that question, because there is no answer to it. He could only reply, "Tell me first, are you under the impression that China has declared war on Afghanistan?" And if you replied in the affirmative, he would proceed to correct your notions. Had you but asked me, "Did the Catholic Church **cut out** the Second Commandment?" a reply could have been given at once. She certainly did not do so.

81. The Protestant Bible gives the Second Commandment as referring to images. But the Catholic Catechism gives it as referring to taking the name of God in vain, omitting the reference to images.

Even the Protestant Bible does not give the Second Commandment as referring to images, though Protestants are usually taught that those words in the First Commandment which refer to images constitute a Second Commandment.

82. The Roman Church omits the Second Commandment, and then breaks up the tenth into two, in order to avoid having only nine.

The reverse is the case. Protestants make the First Commandment into **two,** and then, to escape having **eleven,** turn the ninth and tenth into one! The First Commandment, as given in the Bible, is as follows: "I am the Lord thy God, who brought thee out of the land of Egypt, out of the house of bondage. Thou shalt not have strange Gods before me. Thou shalt not make to thyself a graven thing, nor the likeness of anything that is in Heaven above, or in the earth beneath, nor of those things that are in the waters under the earth. Thou shalt not adore them, nor serve them. I am the Lord thy God, etc." Exodus, XX., 1-6.

83. You are deceiving us. That is not what Catholics are taught. I have a Catholic Catechism which gives the First Commandment as, "I am the Lord thy God; thou shalt not have strange Gods before me." You cut out the reference to images.

In the first place, if we wished to deceive our people, we would be very foolish to give them the full wording of the Commandment in the Douay Version of the Bible, where they could detect the deliberate distortion! In the second place, in the Catechism we give the full substantial sense of the words I have quoted, but in a brief and summarized form which can be easily memorized.

84. And you deny that you have changed the Commandment.

I do. You notice words only, paying little or no attention

to the legal **substance** of those words. To simplify the wording whilst retaining the full sense is certainly not to change the Commandment. If you say, "He is under an obligation not to give expression to his thoughts at the present moment." I do not change the substance of what you say if I repeat to some small child, "He must not speak now." The First Commandment contains within its involved Hebrew amplification two essential points: that we must acknowledge the true God, and that we must avoid false gods. Those two essential points are put briefly and simply in the Catechism for children who are more at home with short and easy sentences.

85. The Commandments do not require such alteration.
The commandments do not. But the **hopeless tangle** most Protestants get into where this First Commandment is concerned shows clearly that it needs to be stated precisely, without any substantial alteration. It is not a question of **words,** but it is a question of **law,** and Catholic children at least know and can clearly state the law.

86. You are violating the text of Scripture. The reference to images is a separate verse.
The numbering of the verses affords no argument. There was **no numerical** distinction of verses in the original Scriptures. Nor did God reveal such distinctions. All who are acquainted with the subject know that Scripture was divided into verses by men some **centuries** after Christ for **greater convenience.** The method of dividing the commandments, however, is not of very great importance. The complaints of Protestants against the Catholic division are rather like that of some modern daughter who would want to spell her name **Smyth,** and complains that her mother spells it **Smith.** But the mother knows best how it should be written, and the mother Church knows best how the Commandments should be numbered.

87. I am interested in Catholic worship. Christ was poor and humble. Yet Catholic ceremonial is full of pomp and display. Does your religion teach humility?
Yes. We are taught to be humble. And Christian humility orders a man to be unassuming and gentle. But it does not forbid a man to worship God as befits God. In fact, the more humble a man is, the more he magnifies and glorifies God, and depreciates self. The Catholic Church says, "God certainly deserves the best we can give Him. Whatever else we may do, let us not be mean in anything where God is concerned. We personally deserve very little, and if by

our gifts God's worship is magnificent and we the poorer, that is how it should be." Christ Himself commended the poor widow for giving all she had to the Temple. Yet he was the one who taught humility.

88. Is it not opposed to the simplicity of His principles?

No. Christ was God, and in the Old Testament God dictated a ceremonial every bit as lavish as Catholic ceremonial. So that it cannot be against His principles. And Christ never condemned ceremonial. He instituted the ceremonial of Baptism with water. With ceremony He breathed upon the Apostles when giving them the power to forgive sins. He came to fulfill the law, not to destroy it. But above all, He founded His Church, giving into her care the guardianship of His religion, and conferring upon her the power to regulate its worship. Whatever the Church has sanctioned in this matter she has done in virtue of the commission given her by her Founder.

89. The ceremonial of the Church shows a great change since the time of Christ.

You won't find the leaves of an oak tree wrapped up inside an acorn. Christ sowed the seed, and said that the small seed He planted would grow into a vast tree. Such growth supposes external changes without loss of identity. Because an acorn has no branches or foliage, will you deny its identity with the tree into which it grows?

90. The Last Supper had no elaborate ceremonial rites, yet look at the Mass today.

The essential rites of the Mass are exactly the same as those of the Last Supper. Remember that before the simple Last Supper Christ had fulfilled the full ceremonial of the Jewish Feast. He ceremoniously washed the disciples' feet. And the growth of the surrounding rites in the Mass has been in accordance with principles dictated by God to the Jews, and by the actions of Christ throughout His public ministry, when He used so many ceremonies in the miracles He worked.

91. Why do priests vest so elaborately when going to say Mass?

In Exodus, XXVIII., 2-3, we read of God's prescriptions of the vestments befitting the dignity of His religion. "Thou shalt make a holy vesture for Aaron thy brother; for glory and for beauty. And thou shalt speak to all the wise of heart, whom I have filled with the spirit of wisdom: that they may make Aaron's vestments, in which he being consecrated may minister to me. And these shall be the vestments that they shall make." Throughout the rest of the chapter God deigns to give the most minute directions as to the various vestments Aaron was to use. Not for a moment would Christ have condemned the principle of vestments after such a sanction by the infinitely wise God. He would be contradicting Himself. There can be nothing wrong with vestments in principle.

92. Christ dressed with the utmost simplicity and talked to God in the most humble places.

Priests also dress with simplicity. They are not always in vestments. As for Christ, He, too, went to the Temple, and took part in its worship, never condemning its ritual. With the establishment of His own Church in fulfillment of the Old Law, He ordained His own priests after the Order of Melchisedech in place of the Levitical Priesthood, and left it to the Church to regulate the ceremonial surrounding the substantial form of worship He had prescribed. As I have said, He would have been the last to condemn a dignified ceremonial, and Anglican Protestants of the High Church group are rapidly trying to resume the vestments prescribed by the Catholic Church, vestments their forefathers so eagerly got rid of; mistakenly, now say the High Church Anglicans.

93. Why the proud display of processions such as those of Eucharistic Congresses?

There is nothing wrong with processions. Christ entered Jerusalem with a procession of the populace crying Hosanna, waving palms and strewing their garments on the roadway, making it as elaborate as they could. And He rebuked those who would have prevented it. Remember that Eucharistic Congresses are not in honor of ourselves, but of Christ, and love of Him suggests that nothing can be too good for Him.

94. When I think of the expense, I think too of the poor, and ask why so much money should be wasted.

Such an objection recalls the words of Judas, "Why was it not sold and given to the poor?" Jn. XII, 5. In any case, the lavish generosity of the Catholic Church in the worship of God does not interfere with her work for the poor. She is the most active of all Churches in that work. No other Church has so many institutions, hospitals, homes, and orphanages; and in many parishes there is a weekly distribution of money and food to the poor through the St. Vincent de Paul or some other society.

95. The ritual of the Roman Church is intricate, mysterious, and sensual, whilst the Gospel is simplicity itself.

The ritual of the Catholic Church is not intricate, save to those who are unfamiliar with it. It is certainly symbolical of many mysteries "hidden from the ages and generations, but now manifested." 1 Col. I, 26. It also involves sensible and visible rites, but in no sense can it be called sensual.

96. Is it not blasphemy to use mingle mangle in baptizing children?

It would be. But no mingle mangle occurs in the baptism of children. Mingle mangle means a meaningless jumble of formulas. But every least item in the baptismal rite is full of meaning and significance. And it is to God's honor and glory to use the holy ceremonies instituted by the Church of Christ with the authority of Christ. Was it mingle mangle when Christ touched the blind man's eyes with spittle before curing him?

97. I went to a Requiem Mass, and was highly amused at the antics of the Priest with his gabble and mumble.

That you were highly amused at a Requiem Mass which you did not understand only proves that you are devoid of the power to sympathize with what is sacred to other people. Had you understood it, and then been amused, there might have been some excuse. You say that the whole ceremony was a gabble and a mumble to you. Were you to attend a session of the German parliament in Berlin, you would probably say the same. "But then," you will reply, "I am not a German. It was all right for them. I knew that well enough, and was not amused, because they were not talking my language, and because it is to be expected that their ways would differ from my ways." So I say in turn, "You are not a Catholic. Every Catholic understands a Requiem Mass. But you should have known that a Protestant would not be likely to understand a Catholic ceremony. That would have checked your amusement. I am a Catholic. But I have never felt like ridiculing the religious services of sincere Protestants.

98. Why does the Catholic Church surround death with gloom, offering the Mass in black vestments, and everything so sad and solemn?

The Catholic Church does not surround death with gloom. But her liturgy is in keeping with man's nature as God intended it to be. Despite all spiritual joy and consolation, whilst hearts are human they break. Even God does not expect us to be hard and inhuman, unmoved when some dear one is taken from us. Our Lord wept with those who mourned the death of Lazarus. And He knew that He was going to bring him back to life again! It is natural to man to find relief in expressing his feelings. St. Paul says, "Be not sorrowful as those who have no hope." But he does not say, "Be not sorrowful." In fact he tells Christians to comfort one another. We do not go up to a man who has just lost his mother, and congratulate him, our faces beaming with joy. That would be inhuman, and the Catholic Church is never inhuman. Near relatives instinctively wear mourning, and dress in black when a loved one dies. Very close friends do the same. And the Catholic Church is the dearest friend any Catholic has, a friend who identifies herself with his feelings in his great loss. It is all in keeping with what is best in man. Death is a solemn thing, and the Catholic Church treats it with solemnity. She does not ask us to sorrow as those who have no hope, but she will not turn a funeral into a wedding feast, and ignore genuine and deep sorrow as if we were so spiritual that we had ceased to be human. We are not in heaven yet.

99. Cathedrals costing thousands are nothing to God. He is a Spirit, and would love just as much without the earthly show.

But man would not love so much! You fail to grasp a fundamental point. It takes two to make a religion, God and Man. God is a pure Spirit, but man is not. Man is a composite of the spiritual and the material. And he must worship God according to his twofold nature. Man not only possesses spiritual thoughts; he gives them expression in speech, writing, music, art and architecture. And, where God is concerned, he dedicates all these things to God's service in religion. God Himself ordered the Jews to do so, commanding the erection of the glorious Temple at Jerusalem. God wants the service, not of half our being, but of our complete being.

100. In Europe I found glorious Cathedrals and pitiable poverty side by side.

The present-day poverty is not due to the Cathedrals which were built long ago by others, who gave their time and services as a voluntary offering to God. The poverty due to modern industrial conditions should not be attributed to buildings erected in other and happier ages. Meantime those beautiful Cathedrals do no harm to men. If the poor pulled them down stone by stone, they could not eat the stones. And even if they could sell them for thirty pieces of silver, the relief would be of a very temporary nature. Believe me, future generations would be just as poor temporally, and much poorer spiritually, with no inspiring Cathedrals.

101. Does crawling up the Scala Santa at Rome on one's knees help save one's soul?

The Scala Santa, or Holy Staircase, consists of twenty-eight marble steps. They are said to have been brought to Rome from Jerusalem by St. Helena, the mother of Constantine, in 326 A. D. At Jerusalem they led up to the one-time court of Pilate, and the feet of Jesus had trodden them as He went down to be crucified by men. With no idea that such an act will of itself save his soul, the Catholic ascends them on his knees out of reverence for Christ, and you have not much reverence and love for Him if you ridicule such a tribute. We Catholics, after all, believe that He is God. We are quite prepared to kiss the very ground whereon He stood. The Pharisees once ridiculed a woman who went on her knees and washed His feet with her tears. But Christ justified her act of loving reverence. Cold Protestantism will never understand the warm-hearted love of Catholicism for the Person of Christ and of all connected with Him. I do not belong to the emotional and demonstrative Latin race. I do not live in the middle ages. I do not suppose I would be ranked as illiterate. Yet whilst in Rome I myself ascended those same stairs on my knees, and I experience no flush of shame as I say so. I have seen a Protestant kiss the pages of the Gospel. He kissed a printed sheet of paper. I admired him for it, and so would you, for we know what it meant to him. I certainly would not ridicule him and ask him sarcastically whether he thought that the smearing of his lips on a piece of paper would help to save his soul! Yet such a remark would be similar to that of a Protestant who suggests that Catholics believe they can be saved by crawling up a staircase on their knees. However you would not have asked such a question had you realized the nature of the subject and the motives prompting such reverence for Christ.